CLAIM the Life

Semester 2

Journey

07   08   09   10   11   12   13   14   15   16—10   9   8   7   6   5   4   3   2   1

Cover Design: Keely Moore

Contents

Glorify

glorify (GLOR-ih-FY) *tr.v..* 1. To give glory, honor, or high praise; exalt. 2. To give glory to, especially through worship.

Write five words or ways that we glorify someone or something. For example, we might honor someone with a certificate for a job well done or give someone a thumbs up!

CODE BREAKER

The Book of Revelation is what is called apocalyptic literature. Written like a code, with lots of strange images, the purpose of this book was to encourage Christians to hold on to the faith in the midst of difficult times of oppression and fear that they were experiencing. Christians of that time would have been able to figure out the "code," but the persecutors would not easily be able to do so.

Here is a portion of the Scripture. See whether you can figure out the code by matching the terms from this passage (in the left column on page 7) to their meanings (in the right column).

And I saw what appeared to be a sea of glass mixed with fire, and those who had conquered the beast and its image and the number of its name, standing beside the sea of glass with harps of God in their hands. And they sing the song of Moses, the servant of God, and the song of the Lamb."

Revelation 15:2-3a

CODE

1. those who had conquered

2. the beast and its image

3. the number of its name

4. sea of glass

5. the song of Moses

6. the Lamb

A. before the throne of God

B. martyrs for the faith who had stayed firm

C. Christ

D. the Roman government

E. rejoicing after miraculous deliverance

F. the Emperor of Rome

Song of the Lamb

"Great and amazing are your deeds,
   Lord God the Almighty!
Just and true are your ways,
   King of the nations!
Lord, who will not fear
   and glorify your name?
For you alone are holy.
   All nations will come
   and worship before you,
for your judgments have been revealed."

—Revelation 15:3b-4

To God Be the Glory

These people loved God so much that they were willing to die for their faith. In doing so, they made an incredible witness to the importance of God. In other words, they glorified God.

We may not be called upon to die for our faith, but we are called to live our witness. How can we glorify God . . .

. . . in our choices? in what we do?

. . . in our attitudes? in the way we do things?

. . . in church?

. . . outside of church?

. . . in taking credit for something we have done well?

All Nations Will Come

What images or lyrics show the extent of all who are glorifying God?

What images or lyrics give you a sense of God's power?

What images or lyrics refer to all who are included and when?

Us too!

What does this information tell you about God?

What are appropriate responses from us to such a God?

Devotion

devotion (dih-VOH-shun) *n.* 1. Loving, often selfless affection and dedication, as to a person or deity; love. 2. Piety. 3. An act of religious observance or prayer, especially when private. 4. A prayer or religious text.

WHAT DOES DEVOTION TO GOD LOOK LIKE?

1 KINGS 8:61

THEREFORE DEVOTE YOURSELVES COMPLETELY TO THE LORD OUR GOD, WALKING IN [GOD'S] STATUTES AND KEEPING [GOD'S] COMMANDMENTS.

(NEW REVISED STANDARD VERSION)

AND MAY YOU . . . ALWAYS BE FAITHFUL TO THE LORD OUR GOD. MAY YOU ALWAYS OBEY [GOD'S] LAWS AND COMMANDS. (NEW LIVING TRANSLATION)

OBEY THE LORD OUR GOD AND FOLLOW [GOD'S] COMMANDS WITH ALL YOUR HEART.
(CONTEMPORARY ENGLISH VERSION)

- Underline words or phrases in these translations that help describe devotion to God. How are they different? How are they the same?

- How would you rewrite this verse, especially in relation to being a young person in the 21st century devoted to God?

Devote yourself to God in everything and listen to all the time has told us.

- Why, do you think, is it important to devote yourself to God this way?

- What are the benefits of such devotion? What happens when we do not devote ourselves to God?

In my Life

school

- What commitments or activities do you do on a regular basis? Circle the words in the right margin that apply to you. Write any others any place on this page.

study

- In which activities does your devotion to God show? In what ways?

practice

chores

- Which activities draw your attention away from God? Why?

church

service

- How can your devotion to God, your passionate faith, become part of all your activities?

youth group

time with

friends

Passionate Faith

Think of your own life. What people, commitments, causes, activities are you devoted to? In other words, to whom or to what do you feel love and loyalty?

I am passionate about

Devoted to God = Passionate Faith

Devotion may not be a word you use much. But do you ever say, or hear others say, "I am passionate about _____"? In this sense, to be passionate is to be emotionally connected, eager, enthusiastic, excited, spirited, intense. Isn't that what it means to be devoted to God? If I am devoted, I am emotionally connected, eager, enthusiastic, excited, spirited, intense about God and about how much God loves me. I am devoted to God's world, God's people, the work God wants me to do in the world. I have a PASSIONATE FAITH.

Let's Get Practical

Think about how devotion to God or a passionate faith in God might be made known in the following situations:

- YOU HAVE TO CHOOSE WHAT TO DO WITH YOUR ALLOWANCE.

- There's no recycling bin for the soda can you just finished. Do you throw the can in the nearest trash can or take it home with you to recycle there?

- You are considering how to be involved in your faith community—helping with the preschool Sunday school, reading Scripture in worship, folding church newsletters.

- A friend tries to push you to do something your parents have forbidden.

- You're out late on Saturday and feel too tired to get up Sunday morning for church.

- YOU'RE INVITED TO AN AFTERNOON AT THE ARCADE OR MALL (WHICHEVER YOU LOVE MORE), BUT YOU ARE ALREADY SIGNED UP FOR A YOUTH GROUP WORK DAY OR MISSION PROJECT.

- A friend wants you to tell the answers to a test you took at an earlier period of the same class.

Beloved

beloved (bih-LUHV-ihd *or* bih-LUHVD) *adj.* Dearly loved; dear to the heart. *n.* One who is dearly loved; one who is dear to the heart.

Beloved, let us love one another, because love is from God; everyone who loves is born of God and knows God.

> Whoever does not love does not know God, for God is love.

God's love was revealed among us in this way: God sent [God's] only Son into the world so that we might live through him.

> In this is love, not that we loved God but that [God] loved us and sent [God's] Son to be the atoning sacrifice for our sins.

Beloved, since God loved us so much, we also ought to love one another.

> No one has ever seen God; if we love one another, God lives in us, and [God's] love is perfected in us.

1 John 4:7-12

Count the Ways

"How do I love thee?
  Let me count the ways.

I love thee to the depth
  and breadth and height

My soul can reach....

—Elizabeth Barrett Browning
"Sonnet 43," from *Sonnets From the Portuguese*

How do you know when someone—family member or friend—loves you? Make a list and count the ways.

Love Song to God

We are God's beloved. How do we show our love for God? Write lyrics, write a poem, make notes, or draw an illustration of at least one way we show God our love.

Am I loved?

Draw a picture or write a description of what it is like to feel that you are not loved or lovable.

Draw a picture or write a description of what it is like to feel that you are loved and lovable.

You Are God's Beloved!

You are God's beloved.

Claim that as an unshakable truth
    for your life.

Live joyfully
    and share that love with others.

Beloved, let us
    love one another.

Decision

decision (dih-SIH-zhuhn) *n.* 1. The passing of judgment on an issue under consideration. 2. The act or process of coming to a conclusion, of making up one's mind. 3. A conclusion; a verdict; a determination.

Decision is something that defines our lives. It is a personal choice based on what we know and feel. Anyone can make a decision, but some decisions will change lives. For example, in Luke 5:1-11, Jesus chose Peter, James, and John; but they also chose him. Because they chose to follow Jesus, they experienced the love and teachings of God. But they also witnessed their Master's death. All that love—and hurt—came because they decided to drop their nets and follow Jesus.

—Madison, age 12

Improv

1. Peter and his Wife

Imagine that you are Peter. You have just come home and must tell your wife about the decision you made today. What will you tell her?

Imagine that you are Peter's wife. He has been fishing all night and all day. You can't wait for him to get home because you have prepared a very special dinner. How will you greet him?

2. Synagogue School

Imagine that you are talking with friends during lunchtime at your synagogue school. Yesterday you were part of the crowd who listened to Jesus, watched as the fishermen brought in the huge catch of fish, and then saw them leave everything to follow Jesus. What will you say to one another?

3. In the Boat

Imagine that you are one of the fisherman who works for Peter. All of you have fished all night alongside Peter and have just helped him haul in the huge net full of fish. Suddenly, Peter leaves to follow Jesus. The rest of you are left to clean a boat load of fish. What will you say to one another?

Claim the Life: Journey, Semester 2

Every Day = Decisions

You make hundreds of decisions every day. Sometimes, in your choices, you have to decide whether you are being a follower of Jesus. The question is, how do you know that you are making faithful decisions? **Philippians 4:8** gives these guidelines:

Whatever is true, whatever is honorable, whatever is just, whatever is pure, whatever is pleasing, whatever is commendable, if there is any excellence and if there is anything worthy of praise, think about these things.

Try using this check list when you have to make a tough decision:

☐ Is it true? (Is your decision based on truth or deceit?)

☐ Is it honorable? (Is this choice seen as the right thing to do?)

☐ Is it just? (Is it as fair as possible to everyone involved?)

☐ Is it pure? (Does the choice make you feel clean or dirty?)

☐ Is it pleasing? (Does it feel like a good thing to do?)

☐ Is it commendable? (Would you recommend this decision to your brother or sister or to your very best friend?)

☐ Is it praiseworthy? (Would others honor and respect you for your decision?)

What to Do?

Greg was having lunch with Camille when Camille asked him whether she could tell him something confidential. Greg said yes, and then Camille told him that she was thinking about committing suicide. She said that life just didn't seem to be worth living anymore.

What are Greg's choices?

1.

2.

3.

4.

Select one of these choices and test it against the guidelines from Scripture listed on page 23.

How does this choice measure up?

LOOKING AHEAD

Look at the week ahead. List some of the choices you will face.

1. _____

2. _____

3. _____

4. _____

5. _____

6. _____

Following Jesus does not always mean making the kind of momentous decisions that Peter made. Sometimes little choices add up to a way of life. Select one of the choices you listed above. How might you make a decision that will be your way of saying, "I will follow Jesus"?

Consider making this one your SMART goal.

Disciple

disciple (dih-SY-puhl) *n.* 1. A follower and learner of a mentor or other wise figure. 2. In Christianity, a follower of Jesus Christ. 3. One who embraces and assists in spreading the teachings of another.

A: Hey, what's with all that stuff?

B: Nothing special. I always have this stuff with me.

A: Don't you ever put it down? It must be hard to do anything else if you don't put it down.

B: Sometimes I think about putting it down, but I don't want to lose any of it.

A: What if you want to do something without having so many distractions?

B: What do you mean?

A: Well, you might want to focus on something really important. Having all of this stuff can get in the way. Maybe you just need to put it down.

B: What if I lose it?

A: Aren't there other things in your life that are more important?

More on the Word

In **Matthew 10:37-38,** Jesus speaks again on the subject of being a disciple. His words clarify the "hate" statement of today's Scripture (**Luke 14:25-33**).

> "Whoever loves father or mother more than me is not worthy of me; and whoever loves son or daughter more than me is not worthy of me" (verse 37).

Jesus doesn't mean that we shouldn't love our families. He does means that we should not love anyone or anything more than we love him.

We can't make bargains with God or put conditions on our loyalties. Jesus gave us the costs of discipleship. Living as disciples is turning our hearts wholly toward God. When something or someone becomes more important in our lives, we are to give them up. Things that might separate us from God might be relationships, material possessions, habits, attitudes, pride, choices, too much of ourself.

This instruction to make Jesus first in our lives seems so simple, yet it can be so very hard to do. Perhaps if we could comprehend the enormity of how much God loves us, we might find it easier for our love of God to take priority in our life.

How do I show my priorities?

Hearts Wholly Toward God

What does the Scripture say to your heart about things you need to love less than you love God?

Are there things or people in your life that draw you away from God, instead of nurturing you and planting you more firmly with God?

Name one possession of yours that distracts you from talking to or listening for God?

What can you do to remind yourself to put God first?

Who can help you live as a disciple?

Knowing that being a fully devoted disciple of Jesus Christ will have a cost to you, are you still willing to follow him?

STUFF   ME   OTHERS

Can You Hear Me, God?

Can you hear me, God?
There's so much going on in my life ;
I can hardly hear myself think!

Can you hear me, God?
I get so side-tracked by my busy schedule
and keeping up with my friends!

Can you find me, God?
I really like having all the latest and the best.
I like my stuff.

Can you see me, God?
I tend to forget
what is most important in my life.

Do you still love me, God?
I'm turning to you now.
I'm asking you:
hold on to me so that I don't get lost.

Can you hear me, God?
I love you.

Disciple

Abstain

abstain (ab-STAYN) intr.*v.* 1. To refrain from something by one's own choice; to refrain deliberately, often with an effort of self-denial from indulging in an action or practice.

If you are guided by the Spirit, you won't obey your selfish desires. The Spirit and your desires are enemies of each other. They are always fighting each other and keeping you from doing what you feel you should. But if you obey the Spirit, the Law of Moses has no control over you.

People's desires make them give in to immoral ways, filthy thoughts, and shameful deeds. They worship idols, practice witchcraft, hate others, and are hard to get along with. People become jealous, angry, and selfish. They not only argue and cause trouble, but they are envious. They get drunk, carry on at wild parties, and do other evil things as well. I told you before, and I am telling you again: No one who does these things will share in the blessings of God's kingdom.

(Galatians 5:16-21, CEV)

SO COOL?

How did the youth on the video define *abstain*? What were some of the phrases they used? What else would you say?

What are things the youth identified as being told to abstain from? What would you add to the list?

The youth talked about a "natural reaction" to being told to abstain. Why, do you think, do people react that way?

Parents are often the ones saying to abstain from something. Why, do you think, do they do that? What did the youth on the video say about why parents do that? Do you agree? How does your relationship with your parents affect how you hear their warnings?

What reasons did the youth give for their own choice to abstain? What would you add? Which of the reasons really caught your attention? Why?

DOES WHAT I DO MATTER?

Look at these things the Scripture identifies as things to abstain from. Add others from the video or your own life. Ask yourself this question:

IF I DON'T ABSTAIN FROM THIS, WHO IS LIKELY TO SUFFER?

Mark an X in the categories on page 33 that apply. You may mark both categories if both of them answer the question.

What Scripture Says We Should Abstain From

act immorally
think filthy thoughts
do shameful deeds
worship idols
practice witchcraft
hate others
act disagreeably
harbor jealous feelings
feel angry
act selfishly
be quarrelsome
cause trouble
feel envy
carry on at wild parties
get drunk
do other evil things such as _____

**Me
(Maybe My Family)**

**Other People I May
or May Not Know**

Love

love (luhv) *n.* 1. Strong affection for another arising out of kinship or personal ties. 2. An intense emotional attachment. 3. The object of deep emotional attachment. 4. An expression of one's affection. 5. Christian affection and charity; agape. 6. Attraction based on sexual desire; a feeling of affection and tenderness by lovers. *tr.v.* 1. To hold dear; cherish. 2. To actively like or desire. *intr.v.* 1. To feel a deep emotional attachment for. 2. To feel affection or experience desire. (*There are too many definitions for* love *to list in this limited space.*)

Galatians 5:13-14

It is absolutely clear that God has called you to a free life. Just make sure that you don't use this freedom as an excuse to do whatever you want to do and destroy your freedom. Rather, use your freedom to serve one another in love; that's how freedom grows. For everything we know about God's Word is summed up in a single sentence: Love others as you love yourself. That's an act of true freedom.

(The Message)

My friends, you were chosen to be free. So don't use your freedom as an excuse to do anything you want. Use it as an opportunity to serve each other with love. All that the Law says can be summed up in the command to love others as much as you love yourself.

(CEV)

There is a love like a small lamp, which goes out when the oil is consumed; or like a stream which dries up when it doesn't rain. But there is a love that is like a mighty spring gushing up out of the earth; it keeps flowing forever, and is inexhaustible.

—Isaac of Nineveh

We can do no great things—only small things with great love.

—Mother Teresa

Loving, like prayer, is a power as well as a process. It's curative. It is creative.

—Zona Gale

If you live for love, you spread kindness and compassion everywhere you go. When you stop believing in your heart, you are but a sterile vessel wandering in the wilderness.

—Francis Hegmeyer

Heart, Soul, Might

What do the following words mean to you in this passage?
Write your own definitions.

HEART = *not just an organ that pumps blood, but something that holds all of your feelings*

SOUL = *your true being that makes you who you are*

MIGHT = *your will to do something*

In your own life, what might it look like to love God with
"heart, soul, and might"? Be specific.

More Than Virtual Love

Love cannot remain by itself—it has no meaning.
Love has to be put into action and that action is service.

—Mother Teresa

Most of us have moments of feeling very loving, especially when our love is "virtual" (not in person). It's funny how much harder it can be to love people when they are with us (and sometimes, annoying or angering us).

Below, write the names of a variety of "neighbors." Some may be people you see every day; others may be far-away neighbors such as people with AIDS in Africa or the homeless in your city. Then fill in how you can "serve in love," as Paul directed.

I will love _____

by _____.

I will love _____

by _____.

I will love _____

by _____.

I will love _____

by _____.

I will love _____

by _____.

I will love _____

by _____.

free to Be

Check all of the statements that you believe define the word "freedom." Add other definitions at the end of the list.

___ Doing whatever you want to do

___ Following Jesus

___ Being free of chains that bind, the opposite of being in prison

___ The power to speak and act for yourself

___ Being physically unrestricted

___ Serving other people

___ Being independent

___ Celebrating on July 4th

___ Being responsible for your own life

___ Making your own choices

___ Making your own choices as a Christian

___

___

___

___

___

Get Specific

Moses, Jesus, and Paul all emphasized loving God and loving neighbor. Our love must be more than a nice idea. Write in the spaces below some specific ways you can put love into action.

Specific ways I can show that I follow Jesus' five commandments to love:

Love God

Love neighbor

Love yourself

Love one another

Love your enemies

Action

action (AK-shuhn) *n.* 1. The state or process of doing. 2. Something done or accomplished; a deed. 3. Organized activity to accomplish an objective. 4. Behavior; conduct; initiative.

We know love by this, that [Christ] laid down his life for us—and we ought to lay down our lives for one another. How does God's love abide in anyone who has the world's goods and sees a brother or sister in need and yet refuses to help?

Little children, let us love, not in word or speech, but in truth and action.

1 John 3:16-18 (NRSV)

This is how we have come to understand and experience love: Christ sacrificed his life for us. This is why we ought to live sacrificially for our fellow believers, and not just be out for ourselves. If you see some brother or sister in need and have the means to do something about it but turn a cold shoulder and do nothing, what happens to God's love? It disappears. And you made it disappear.

My dear children, let's not just talk about love; let's practice real love.

1 John 3:16-18 (*Message*)

BE A CHRISTIAN

Who are the "needy" you know? ("Needy" does not necessarily mean being in financial need; emotional, physical, social, and spiritual needs count too.) List them.

Then think about what God has given you that could help care for those needs. List resources (time, service, money, knowledge, skill, for example) or attributes (being a good listener, being a good researcher, being supportive with your presence, being a good communicator, being a good organizer, for example) that you have that could help.

WHO IS NEEDY?	WHAT RESOURCE OR ATTRIBUTES DO I HAVE THAT COULD HELP?
_____	_____
_____	_____
_____	_____

When you write your **SMART** goal, think about this information. How could you put your resources or attributes in action to help the needy?

SACRIFICIAL LOVE

THIS IS HOW WE'VE COME TO UNDERSTAND AND EXPERIENCE LOVE: CHRIST SACRIFICED HIS LIFE FOR US. THIS IS WHY WE OUGHT TO LIVE SACRIFICIALLY.

1 JOHN 3:16A (MESSAGE)

WHAT'S THE SOURCE OF LOVE FOR CHRISTIANS?

WHAT DOES THE SCRIPTURE ASSUME ABOUT PERSONS WHO DO NOT HAVE GOD'S LOVE LIVING WITH THEM?

WHAT DOES IT MEAN TO LIVE SACRIFICIALLY? HOW DOES HAVING GOD'S LOVE RESIDING IN US ENABLE US TO GIVE TO THE NEEDY?

Four Kinds of Love

How have you experienced these four kinds of love? Who loved you, or whom did you love? What actions demonstrated this love? (It's OK to use examples from others you know or from TV or the movies.)

Category	Meaning	Who or Whom	Action
Affection	family fondness	_____	_____
Philia	friendship	_____	_____
Eros	being in love	_____	_____
Agape	reflection of God's love	_____	_____

TALK TO ACTION

What are some ways you measure the truth and sincerity of . . .

. . . your love for others?

. . . someone else's love for you?

. . . God's love for you?

. . . your love for God?

Honesty

> **honesty** (AHN-uh-stee) *n.* 1. The quality or condition of being honest; integrity. 2. Truthfulness; sincerity. 3. Fairness and straightforwardness of conduct. 4. Uprightness of character or action.

CHEATING—WHAT DO YOU THINK?

Do think that cheating is ever justified? You know that the answer is supposed to be "no," but.... Put a checkmark in the box that best shows how you feel about each situation below.

	It's OK	Maybe	Sometimes	Never
1. Cheat on a test				✓
2. Lie to your parents				✓
3. Shoplift				✓
4. Download music illegally	✓	✓		
5. Copy someone else's homework or exam answers				✓
6. Make a promise you don't intend to keep				✓
7. Tell a "white lie"				✓
8. Ignore a library fine			✓	
9. Keep all of the change when given too much		✓		
10. Borrow something without first asking permission			✓	

One-Liners

The Book of Proverbs in the Old Testament contains a whole series of one-liners about living a good life. Some sound funny to us, and others are very familiar. Here's what **Proverbs 24:26** says about honesty:

"One who gives an honest answer gives a kiss on the lips." (NRSV)

"An honest answer is like a warm hug." (The Message)

Make a Proverb

In the space below, write at least three proverbs of your own, describing what honesty is like.

Honesty is like

Honesty is like

Honesty is like

PARAPHRASING SCRIPTURE

Read Deuteronomy 25:13-16.

What, do you think, did this Scripture mean to the people who first heard it?

What does it mean to you? How does it apply now?

Rewrite the Scripture in your own words, using examples from your world.

Honesty is something we decide to practice. Honesty is the ability to tell the truth even if it is hard. The level of honesty shown by a person factors into what kind of person that individual is—a responsible one or a deceitful one. Honesty is almost always portrayed as a good thing, but can also be taken or dealt with dangerously. Deuteronomy 25:13-16 says that to know God and dwell in the land God is giving the people, they must be honest. To obey God in every aspect, don't do something you shouldn't; then you won't be tempted to be dishonest about it later. Honesty and trust are the two things people depend on to make things better, and you should never mess with that trust between you and God.

—Madison, age 12

Hospitality

hospitality (HOS-pih-TAL-ih-tee) *n.* 1. The act of making someone feel welcome, comfortable, even special. 2. The act of attending to the needs of a guest. 3. The act of inviting a person into your space (classroom, youth group space, home, neighborhood, community, congregation, and so on). 4. The act of receiving and entertaining a stranger or guest, without expectation of reward. 5. The act of receiving a guest with kindness and generosity.

Let mutual love continue. Do not neglect to show hospitality to strangers, for by doing that some have entertained angels without knowing it.

Hebrews 13:1-2

LET'S DO IT!

Here are three occasions that call for hospitality. Make notes about what you and your group could do to be hospitable. Note as well what would be inhospitable, what you want to avoid. Consider the questions below as you decide what to do.

Plan a party

Whom will you invite? Why? Who will be left out? Why?

What can you do to be sure everyone will feel noticed and special?

Welcome a new person to school

How have you been welcomed when you didn't know anyone?

What else might you and your friends do beyond the first welcome?

Include someone who "shows up"

What plan do you think your youth group or Sunday school class should have for such occasions?

What if someone you don't like at school shows up here?

Stranger or Not a Stranger?

Yes No

__ __ next-door neighbors

__ __ your English teacher

__ __ your aunt or uncle

__ __ new student at school

__ __ the student whose locker is next to yours

__ __ checkout clerk at a grocery store

__ __ visitor to your youth group

__ __ your brother or sister's friends

__ __ waiters and waitresses

__ __ people with disabilities

__ __ principal of your school

__ __ your school's custodian

__ __ homeless people

__ __ telemarketers

__ __ elderly people

__ __ cheerleaders

__ __ shy people

__ __ smart kids

__ __ Muslims

__ __ Jews

__ __ police

Claim the Life: Journey, Semester 2

WE FEEL AWKWARD ...

Sometimes it feels really weird to welcome someone new to your group of friends. One youth group felt that hospitality was really important, so they adopted the slogan "We feel awkward so you don't have to." They welcome new people even though it sometimes feels uncomfortable while they are doing it. They have decided that it's really important for new people to feel comfortable when they visit youth group. So they put themselves in an awkward position in order to help the new person feel at ease.

"We feel awkward so you don't have to."

Brokenness

brokenness (BROH-kuhn-nes) *n.* 1. The condition of being completely subdued; humbled. 2. The feeling or showing of sorrow and remorse for a sin or shortcoming; contriteness.

Psalm 51:16-17

16 For you [God] have no delight in sacrifice

    if I were to give a burnt offering, you would not be pleased.

17 The sacrifice acceptable to God is a broken spirit;

    a broken and contrite heart, O God, you will not despise.

(NRSV)

16 Going through the motions doesn't please you, a flawless performance is nothing to you.

17 I learned God-worship when my pride was shattered. Heart-shattered lives ready for love don't for a moment escape God's notice.

(Message)

THAT BROKEN PLACE

Write (or talk) about a time you really felt that you were at a low point in your life. How did you get to that place? How did you feel? How did you recover? These are some questions to help you get started:

- What is the mood created by the song? When have you had those feelings?

- When have you ever tried your best at something but didn't succeed?

- When have you felt totally exhausted but found yourself unable to sleep?

- What do you have that, if you lost it, you would not be able to replace it?

- When have you received something you really wanted and then discovered that it wasn't what you really needed?

- When have you loved someone, but your love "went to waste"?

- When have you had tears streaming down your face?

Broken Place

Totally letting go emotionally usually means that something in our life is broken. It may be a broken relationship or perhaps even a death. It may be failure in something we really wanted.

- Is there anything in your life right now that you would describe as broken?

We each come to our broken place for different reasons and from different circumstances. It is in that "broken" place, though, that we find God waiting for us with open arms.

- As you pray, see yourself handing over to God the brokenness in your life. Know that you are being held in God's hands. Only God, the Great Physician, the Master Potter, can heal and reshape your life into something whole and beautiful again.

Re-Usables

Throwing away things when they break is such a temptation even when the breakage isn't major. However, if we think first, often we can find new uses for broken things. For example:

Item: A Broken Plate

New Uses

⟶Break it some more and then use the little pieces to make custom jewelry. (Put backings on two similar pieces to make a pair of earrings or hot glue several pieces to a piece of heavy cardboard with a pin back glued to it to make a brooch.)

⟶Glue the pieces around an old picture frame.

⟶Tie the ribbon of a helium balloon around a piece of the plate for a cheap weight to keep the balloon from floating away.

Are you getting the idea? Now you try coming up with ideas for new ways to use some broken things, such as balloons, a mailbox, a milk carton, a stereo, a telephone, a seashell, and other items you can think of.

Hardship

> **hardship** (HARD-ship) *n.* 1. The state of being deprived or of suffering. 2. A cause of deprivation or suffering. 3. Difficulty.

JOSEPH'S HARDSHIPS

Read the passages below and record Joseph's hardships. At the end of each section, identify ways in which God was at work. Finally, identify what Joseph saw as his blessings.

Genesis 37:2-4, 8

Genesis 37:19-24

Genesis 37:27-28

Genesis 37:31-33

Where do you see God?

Genesis 39:1-6a

Genesis 39:6b-19

Where do you see God?

Genesis 40:2, 9-14, 23

Genesis 41:1a, 9, 14-16, 46

Where do you see God?

What does Joseph identify as two blessings from God?
(Genesis 41:46-52)

Been There, Done That—Didn't Like the T-shirt!

How has your faith helped? or not helped? How have you
sensed God's presence or seen God at work in the
experience? or not? What impact has the hardship had on
your relationship with God?

Generosity

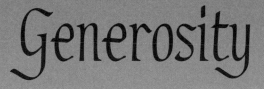

> **generosity** (JEN-uh-ROS-ih-tee) *n.* 1. The quality or fact of ready, willing, kind, and unrestrained giving. 2. Readiness or freeness in giving. 3. Freedom from meanness or smallness of mind or character. 4. Relative degree of plentifulness.

If there is among you anyone in need, a member of your community,...do not be hard-hearted or tight-fisted toward your needy neighbor....Give liberally and be ungrudging when you do so, for on this account the LORD your God will bless you in all your work and in all that you undertake. Since there will never cease to be some in need on the earth, I therefore command you, "Open your hand to the poor and needy neighbor in your land."
(Deuteronomy 15:7, 10-11)

Giving God's Way

With what attitude does God say you should give to others?

How would government and church funds be treated differently if those persons making decisions were committed to following God's command?

What will happen when you give in the way God commands?

How can you give appropriately if you don't know the poor and their needs? How can you better know the poor and needy in your land?

- Do you think that it's easier to give away your money if you have a lot of it? Why, or why not?

- If you were to receive $10,000 tomorrow, what portion of it would you give away to whom? Why? Is your answer an example of biblical generosity? Why, or why not?

CHART THE SCRIPTURES

Look up the following verses and fill in the chart's blanks wit the answer to this question: What does this verse say about giving?

Deuteronomy 15:7-11

Matthew 5:42

Matthew 6:3

Mark 12:41-44

Luke 6:38

Luke 12:33

Luke 18:22

1 Corinthians 13:3

2 Corinthians 9:7-8

Identify two or three recurring themes among these Scriptures.

A MATTER OF THE HEART

Being generous towards the poor and needy in your land is more about the state of your heart, not about how much money you have. How willing are you to give of your time, your friendship, your prayers, your service? Below, write ways you could generously bless those with the following needs:

1. A SINGLE MOTHER WHO WORKS TWO JOBS AND HAS TWO CHILDREN, AGES 8 AND 6

2. AN OLDER CHURCH MEMBER WHO IS BLIND AND CANNOT DRIVE TO CHURCH

3. A MEMBER OF YOUR COMMUNITY WHO HAS BEEN LAID OFF FROM WORK AND CANNOT PAY THE RENT

4. THE LOCAL HUMANE SHELTER THAT NEEDS FOOD, MEDICINE, AND SUPPLIES FOR THE MORE THAN 50 ANIMALS IT HOUSES

5. CHILDREN AT THE LOCAL ELEMENTARY SCHOOL WHO SCORED BELOW PROFICIENCY LEVEL ON THE LAST STATEWIDE ACHIEVEMENT TEST

7. YOUR PARENTS, WHO ARE FIGHTING ABOUT THE FAMILY'S INCOME AND MONTHLY BUDGET

6. YOUR BEST FRIEND WHO IS BEING PRESSURED BY HER BOYFRIEND TO HAVE SEX

- What, do you think, does it mean to "be generous" in each of the situations in the hearts?

- Choose one or two of the scenarios. How would someone lacking generosity approach each situation? Why?

- What, for you, is the situation most difficult to view in light of being generous? Why?

Budget Worksheet

Your team is in charge of allocating the state's funds to various state agencies. How will you decide which groups get what amount of money? Read the information about the seven needs. Then write on page 69 how much money, if any, you will give to each agency. Take notes as you work; you will need to make your case for your choices to convince the other teams.

Together the agencies have requested **$1,100,000.** You have only **$750,000** to disperse among them.

1. State Employees

These persons staff the state offices. They have not had a raise in three years and are threatening to walk out if they do not get at least $100,000 in this year's budget. This money would fund employee raises and the renovation of the employee cafeteria. The median salary for state employees is $45,000 per year. Many are career employees, having worked for the state for at least twenty years. About 35% don't have a college degree; 45% are single parents.

Your thoughts:

2. Schools

Your state's public schools desperately need qualified teachers, new textbooks and technology, buildings, and transportation. For the second year, students in your state have scored in the bottom third for reading and math proficiency in the nation. Qualified teachers move out of state or travel across state lines to find jobs and better pay. More and more students are going to private school, being home schooled, or dropping out because public education is substandard. School officials say that they need at least $200,000 to make improvements in the education system. They claim a poor education system affects every aspect of life, including lost new business ventures and increased teen pregnancy and crime rates.

Your thoughts:

3. Drug Task Force
Keeping kids off drugs and rehabilitating drug addicts are primary goals of your governor. The drug task force has done remarkable work in the last few years. Drug addiction has dropped 30% and there were 100 fewer murders in your state this year as opposed to last year—a statistic directly related to the drop in drug addiction and availability of drugs. The drug task force works closely with the state police and education systems to put more cops on the streets and in the schools. The task force also has an in-school program that teaches kids about the dangers of drugs. Operating for five years, more than 50 new state jobs have been created under the drug task force department. The task force is asking for $100,000, earmarking it for "education"; but an investigative news journalist has recently reported that the director wants a new state-issued car.

Your thoughts:

4. Lottery
The state lottery has been operating in your state for about two years. The money generated provides $1000 scholarships for students with GPAs of 3.2 or higher. The lottery director makes a $150,000 annual salary. She has asked for a raise of an additional $50,000.

Your thoughts:

5. Police and Fire
The state police and fire groups employ more than 5,000 employees across the state. They are requesting $200,000 for maintenance of emergency vehicles.

Your thoughts:

6. State Services Agency

This agency operates several shelters around the state, serving critical needs. The homeless shelter serves three hot meals, provides warm beds, and a hot shower to more than 200 men daily. They also sponsor a job locator program, having acquired permanent work and housing for more than 3,000 persons during the ten years they've been operating. The Women in Crisis shelter provides temporary housing and protection for women and children seeking to escape abusive relationships. More than 100 women are served there daily. The Agency also works with churches and other organizations to provide emergency medical care, hunger relief, and counseling services to men, women, and children on an as-needed basis throughout the state.

The agency has reached a critical funding shortage, due to a lack of private contributions. They also gave extra financial and resource support to victims of Hurricane Katrina in 2005 and are still feeling the effects of offering that help. The agency says that it needs at least $300,000 to keep the doors open and to keep most programs running. More money would mean that the agency could replenish those resources tapped out by the Katrina crisis. Otherwise, the agency will need to shut down programs and turn away the needy.

Your thoughts:

7. Trash Removal

The state trash removal agency is a newly created agency that will work part time to remove debris from the interstate roadways. Last year, more than 300 fatal car accidents were caused by vehicles either hitting or swerving to miss debris on the roads. Three persons will be hired to travel the roads (in the state's three main regions) picking up trash. The agency says that it will take $150,000 to employ the three people and operate three vehicles.

Your thoughts:

Budget Proposal

Agencies	Requested	Allocated
1. State Employees	$100,000	
2. Schools	$200,000	
3. Drug Task Force	$100,000	
4. Lottery	$50,000	
5. Police and Fire	$200,000	
6. State Service Agency	$300,000	
7. Trash Removal	$150,000	
Total	$1,100,000	

Our Rationale

Below are our reasons for how we assigned the funds:

1.

2.

3.

4.

5.

6.

7.

Fruitful

fruitful (FROOT-fuhl) *adj.* 1. Yielding or producing fruit. 2. Conducive to an abundant yield. 3. Causing to bear in abundance. 4. Abundantly productive. 5. Producing results.

"I am the true vine, and my Father is the vinegrower. He removes every branch in me that bears no fruit. Every branch that bears fruit he prunes to make it bear more fruit. You have already been cleansed by the word that I have spoken to you. Abide in me as I abide in you. Just as the branch cannot bear fruit by itself unless it abides in the vine, neither can you unless you abide in me. I am the vine, you are the branches. Those who abide in me and I in them bear much fruit, because apart from me you can do nothing."

(John 15:1-5)

Two Branches

Look at the two branches. What do you notice? What are the differences? Which, do you think, will bear more weight? Why?

After the experiment, which branch could bear more fruit? Why?

Branch Tending

"I am the vine, you are the branches. Those who abide in me and I in them bear much fruit" (John 15:5).

Below and on the next page are some practices of the faith that will help you abide in Jesus and grow stronger in your connection to the Source of fruitfulness. Underline the ones that you are already doing faithfully. Put a check by ones you have done occasionally. Circle one or two that you would like to learn more about or to try soon.

Prayer

Keeping the Sabbath

Meditation

Devotional Reading

Lectio Divina

Bible Study

Self-denial

Stillness and Silence

Singing From the Soul

Living Simply

Holy Communion

Worship

Christian Fellowship

Acts of Justice

Acts of Care

Being the Body of Christ

Participating in Sunday School

Humility

> **humility** (hyoo-MIL-ih-tee) *n.* 1. The quality or condition of being humble; of reflecting, expressing or offering in a spirit of deference or submission. 2. The state of not having an excessive appreciation of one's own worth or virtue; the state of being without conceit or ego.

When [Jesus] noticed how the guests chose the places of honor, he told them a parable.

"When you are invited by someone to a wedding banquet, do not sit down at the place of honor, in case someone more distinguished than you has been invited by your host; and the host who invited both of you may come and say to you, 'Give this person your place,' and then in disgrace you would start to take the lowest place. But when you are invited, go and sit down at the lowest place, so that when your host comes, he may say to you, 'Friend, move up higher'; then you will be honored in the presence of all who sit at the table with you. For all who exalt themselves will be humbled, and those who humble themselves will be exalted."

Luke 14:7-11 (NRSV)

"What I am saying is, if you walk around with your nose in the air, you're going to end up flat on your face. But if you're content to be simply yourself, you will become more than yourself."—Jesus

(Luke 14:11, Message)

MOVE OVER

Spend a few minutes reflecting on this activity. Was there a strategy? How did you get to sit in the seat of honor?

How did people end up in the seat of humiliation? How often did those really trying to get the seat of honor end up in the seat of humiliation?

What do you think of how the game ended?

What Would Jesus Say?

After reading the Scripture passages on page 74,
write the advice you think Jesus would give to Simone.

What, do you think, would Jesus say to Chuck?

What, do you think, would Jesus say to you?

Light

light (lyt) *n.* 1. Source of illumination that brightens, clarifies, guides, or inspires. 2. A person who inspires or is adored by another. tr.*v.* To signal, direct, or guide.

"You are the light of the world. A city built on a hill cannot be hid. No one after lighting a lamp puts it under the bushel basket, but on the lampstand, and it gives light to all in the house. In the same way, let your light shine before others, so that they may see your good works and give glory to your Father in heaven."

(Matthew 5:14-16)

Living in Darkness

Describe a time when you have or someone you know has been in darkness. How did that feel? What were some of the results of being in darkness?

"I have come as light into the world, so that everyone who believes in me should not remain in the darkness."

—Jesus Christ (John 12:46)

To Hide or Shine

- Why, do you think, do Christian youth sometimes hide their light?

- What are some ways you, as an individual, can let your light shine so that others will see God?

- How is the church like a "city on hill"? What are some ways the church can shine light in the world? Give some examples.

- How does being part of the church help us shine light for others?

- Do you want people to know who did the good deed for them or who provided what they needed? Why, or why not? Think about yourself as an individual then about the church as you discuss this question.

- Why is it important, sometimes, that persons *do* know who helped them? Give an example.

- When Christians help others, on whom should the spotlight shine?

Journey

faith journey (JUHR-nee) *n.* Choosing to grow closer and closer to God; traveling through life as a follower of Jesus Christ; refusing to stay put and stop growing in faith.

Which of the words or SMART goals in this study mean the most to you? Why?

What steps are you ready to take as you continue your journey as a disciple of Jesus Christ?